PIANO · VOCAL · GUITAR

THE **BIG** BOOK

FOLK POP ROCK

ISBN 0-634-08068-7

HAL·LEONARD®
CORPORATION
7777 W. BLUEMOUND RD. P.O. BOX 13819 MILWAUKEE, WI 53213

Visit Hal Leonard Online at
www.halleonard.com

CONTENTS

ALISON

Words and Music by
ELVIS COSTELLO

ALL I KNOW

Words and Music by
JIMMY WEBB

that's all ___ I know. ___

AMERICAN TUNE

Words and Music by
PAUL SIMON

And I dreamed I was dy - ing, I dreamed that my soul rose un - ex - pect - ed - ly, And look - ing back down at me, smiled re - as - sur - ing - ly. And I dreamed I was fly - ing, And high up a - bove my eyes could clear - ly see the Sta - tue of

al-right, it's al-right.___ You can't be for - ev - er blessed.___

Still, to-mor-row's goin' to be an-oth-er work - ing day, And I'm

try - ing to get___ some rest,___ That's all I'm try - ing, to get some___

rest.

ritard.

AMERICAN PIE

Words and Music by
DON McLEAN

Additional Lyrics

2. Now for ten years we've been on our own,
   And moss grows fat on a rollin' stone
   But that's not how it used to be
   When the jester sang for the king and queen
   In a coat he borrowed from James Dean
   And a voice that came from you and me
   Oh and while the king was looking down,
   The jester stole his thorny crown
   The courtroom was adjourned,
   No verdict was returned
   And while Lenin read a book on Marx
   The quartet practiced in the park
   And we sang dirges in the dark
   The day the music died
   We were singin'... bye-bye... etc.

3. Helter-skelter in the summer swelter
   The birds flew off with a fallout shelter
   Eight miles high and fallin' fast,
   it landed foul on the grass
   The players tried for a forward pass,
   With the jester on the sidelines in a cast
   Now the half-time air was sweet perfume
   While the sergeants played a marching tune
   We all got up to dance
   But we never got the chance
   'Cause the players tried to take the field,
   The marching band refused to yield
   Do you recall what was revealed
   The day the music died
   We started singin'... bye-bye... etc.

4. And there we were all in one place,
   A generation lost in space
   With no time left to start again
   So come on, Jack be nimble, Jack be quick,
   Jack Flash sat on a candlestick
   'Cause fire is the devil's only friend
   And as I watched him on the stage
   My hands were clenched in fists of rage
   No angel born in hell
   Could break that Satan's spell
   And as the flames climbed high into the night
   To light the sacrificial rite
   I saw Satan laughing with delight
   The day the music died
   He was singin'... bye-bye... etc.

ANNIE'S SONG

Words and Music by
JOHN DENVER

ANTICIPATION

Words and Music by
CARLY SIMON

AT SEVENTEEN

Words and Music by
JANIS IAN

BEST OF MY LOVE

Words and Music by JOHN DAVID SOUTHER,
DON HENLEY and GLENN FREY

Moderately slow

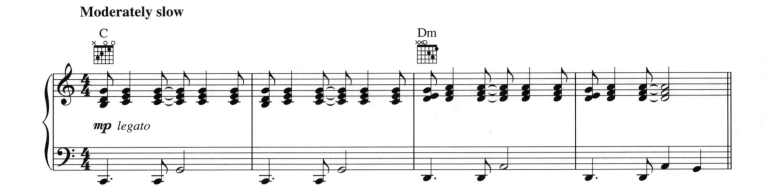

Ev-er-y night ___ I'm ly-in' in bed, ___ hold-in' you close ___ in my
Beau-ti-ful fac-es and loud emp-ty plac-es, look at the way that we

dreams; ___ think-in' a-bout ___ all the things that we ___ said ___ and
live; ___ wast-in' our time ___ on cheap talk and wine

BIRD ON THE WIRE
(Bird on a Wire)

Words and Music by
LEONARD COHEN

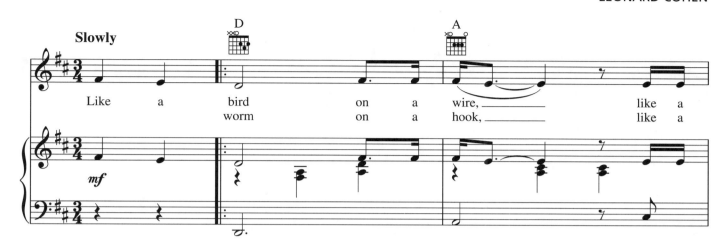

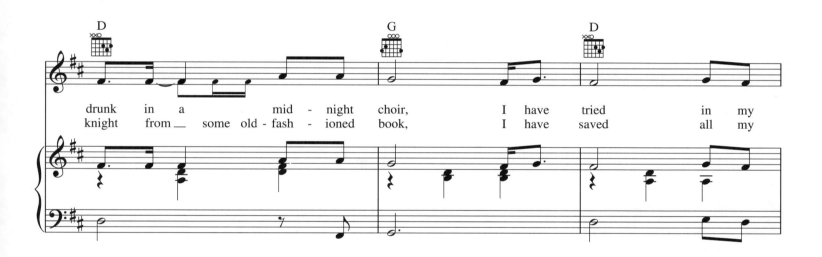

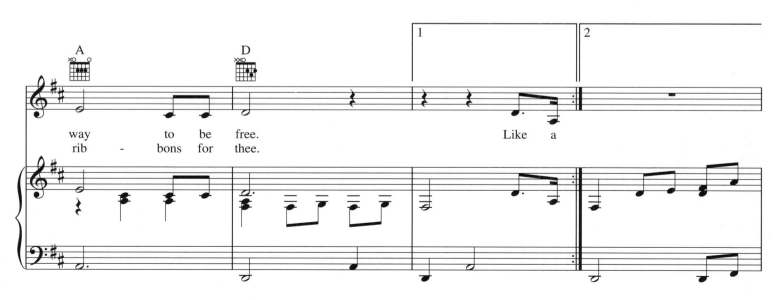

If I, if I have been un-kind,

I hope that you can just let it go by.

If I, if I have been un-true,

I hope you know it was nev-er to you. More like a

she cried to me, "Hey, why not ask for more?" More like a bird on the wi - re, ___ like a drunk in a mid - night choir, I have tried in my way to be free. ___

BLACKBIRD

Words and Music by JOHN LENNON
and PAUL McCARTNEY

CHICAGO

Words and Music by
GRAHAM NASH

* *Male vocal written at actual pitch.*

CHUCK E'S IN LOVE

Words and Music by
RICKIE LEE JONES

COTTON FIELDS
(The Cotton Song)

Words and Music by
HUDDIE LEDBETTER

CLOSER TO FINE

Words and Music by
EMILY SALIERS

Additional Lyrics

2. Well, darkness has a hunger that's insatiable, and lightness has a call that's hard to hear.
   I wrap my fear around me like a blanket.
   I sailed my ship of safety till I sank it.
   I'm crawling on your shores.

3. I went to the Doctor of Philosophy with a poster of Rasputin and a beard down do his knee.
   He never did marry or see a B - Grade movie.
   He graded my performance, he said he could see through me.
   I spent four years prostrate to the higher mind, got my paper and I was free.

4. I stopped by a bar at three A.M. to seek solace in a bottle, or possibly a friend.
   I woke up with a headache like my head against a board, twice as cloudy as I'd been the night before.
   And I went in seeking clarity.

CONSTANT CRAVING

Words and Music by k.d. lang
and BEN MINK

* Chords in parenthesis indicate those played when capo is used.

DARK HOLLOW

Words and Music by
BILL BROWNING

I'd rath-er be in some dark

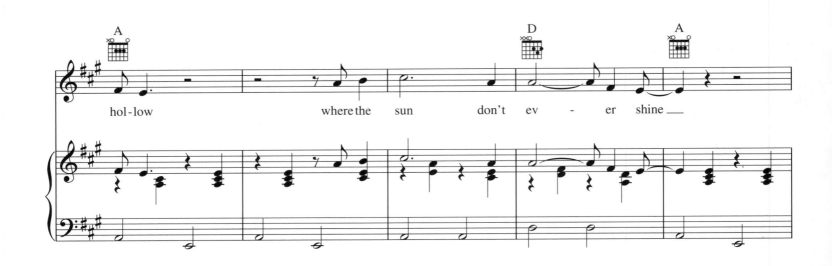

hol-low where the sun don't ev-er shine

than to be home a-lone, in some big cit-y know-in' that you're gone, would in a

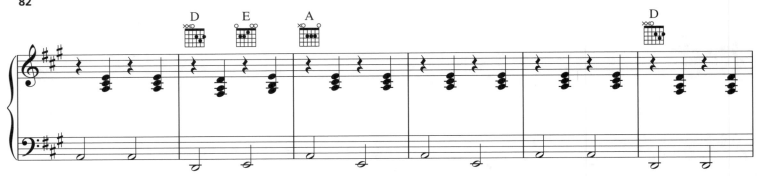

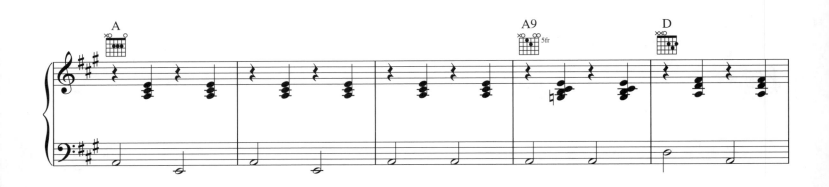

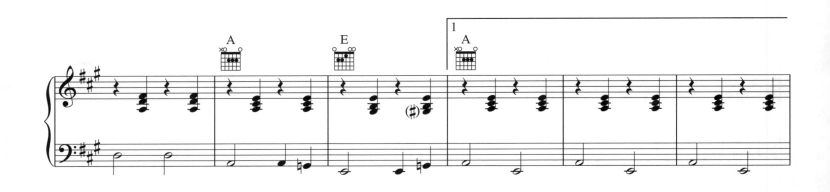

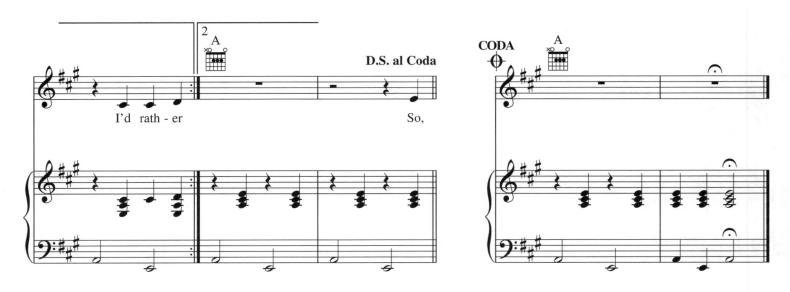

I'd rath - er

So,

DIMMING OF THE DAY

Written by
RICHARD THOMPSON

This old house—

— have come   is fall-ing down— a -round— my——— ears;—
— you   to keep— us far— a - part,—
on the street— in com - pa - ny.—

* Recorded a half step higher

DO YOU BELIEVE IN MAGIC

Words and Music by
JOHN SEBASTIAN

makes you feel hap-py like an old time mov-ie. I'll tell you 'bout the mag-ic and it'll

free your soul But it's like try-in' to tell a stran-ger 'bout a rock and roll.___

2. If you be-lieve in mag - ic   don't you both-er to choose,   If it's
3. (If you be-lieve in mag) - ic   come a - long with   me.   We'll___

DON'T LET THE RAIN COME DOWN

(Crooked Little Man) (Crooked Little House)

Words and Music by ERSEL HICKY
and ED E. MILLER

Moderate Calypso

DUST IN THE WIND

Words and Music by
KERRY LIVGREN

Moderate Folk style

Ev - 'ry - thing _ is dust in the wind.
wind.)

Repeat and Fade

Optional Ending

poco rit.

EIGHT MILES HIGH

Words and Music by ROGER McGUINN,
DAVID CROSBY and GENE CLARK

EVERYBODY'S TALKIN'

(Echoes)
from MIDNIGHT COWBOY

Words and Music by
FRED NEIL

EVERYTHING I OWN

Words and Music by
DAVID GATES

FAST CAR

Words and Music by
TRACY CHAPMAN

buy a big house and live in the sub-urbs. take your fast car and keep on driv-ing.

D.S. al Coda

CODA

You got a fast car. Is it fast e-nough so you can fly a-way?

You got-ta make a de-ci-sion, you leave to-night or live and die this way.

Play 3 times

A FATHER AND A SON

Words and Music by
LOUDON WAINWRIGHT III

FLAKE

Words and Music by
JACK JOHNSON

The hard-er that you try, ba-by, the hard-er you'll

fall, e - ven with all ___ the money in ___ the whole ___ wide world. ___

Please, please, please don't pass me, please, please, please don't pass me, please please, please don't pass me by. ___

GET CLOSER

Words and Music by JAMES SEALS
and DASH CROFTS

Moderately, with a strong beat
Tacet

Dar-lin', if you want me to be _____ clos-er to you, _____ get clos-er to me..

Dar-lin', if you want me to be _____ clos-er to you,_

_____ get clos-er to me._____ Dar-lin', if you want me to love,_

HAPPY TOGETHER

Words and Music by GARRY BONNER
and ALAN GORDON

HELLO, IT'S ME

Words and Music by
TODD RUNDGREN

HERE COMES THE SUN

Words and Music by
GEORGE HARRISON

Here comes _ the sun, ___ doo da doo doo,

here comes _ the sun, ___ and I say, "It's all ___ right."

Here comes _ the sun, _____ here comes _ the sun, _____ and I say, "It's all ____ right."

To Coda ⊕

Sun, sun, sun, here it comes.

D.S. al Coda

HELP ME MAKE IT THROUGH THE NIGHT

Words and Music by
KRIS KRISTOFFERSON

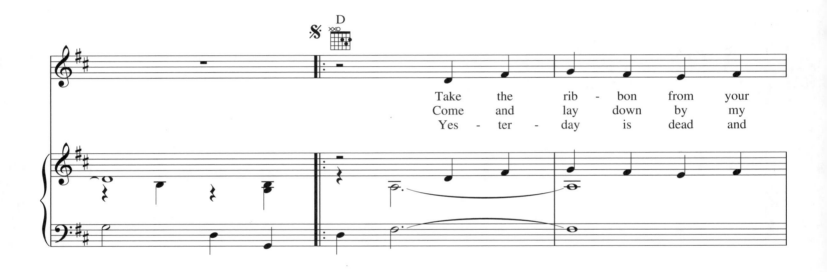

Take the rib - bon from your
Come and lay down by my
Yes - ter - day is dead my and

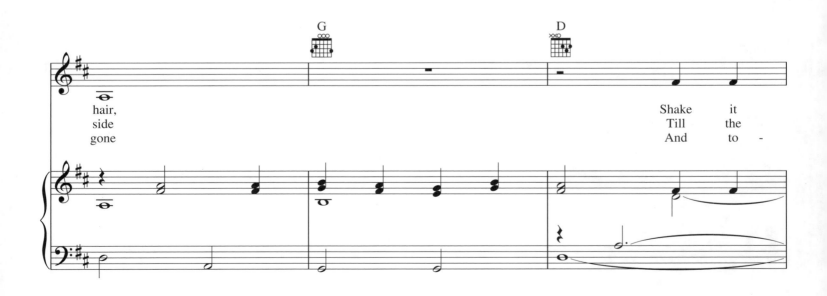

hair,
side
gone

Shake it
Till the
And to -

HER TOWN TOO

Words and Music by JOHN DAVID SOUTHER,
JAMES TAYLOR and ROBERT WACHTEL

HONEYCOMB

Words and Music by
BOB MERRILL

Additional Lyrics

2. Now have you heard tell how they made a bee?
   Then tried a hand at a green, green tree.
   So the tree was made and I guess you've heard,
   Next they made a bird.
   Then they went around lookin' everywhere,
   Takin' love from here and from there,
   And they stored it up in a little cart,
   For my honey's heart.
   Chorus

HOW LONG

Words and Music by
PAUL CARRACK

I FEEL THE EARTH MOVE

Words and Music by
CAROLE KING

Moderate Rock

I feel the earth move under my feet; I feel the sky tum-bl-in' down. I feel my heart start to trem-bl-in' when-ev-er you're a-round.

I'LL HAVE TO SAY I LOVE YOU IN A SONG

Words and Music by
JIM CROCE

I'VE BEEN TO MEMPHIS

Words and Music by
LYLE LOVETT

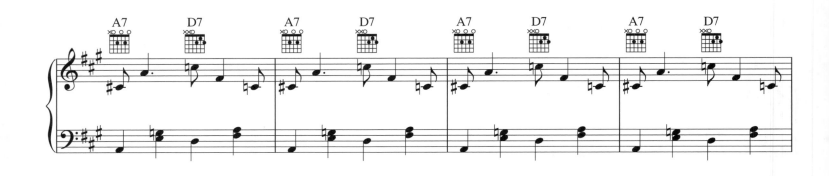

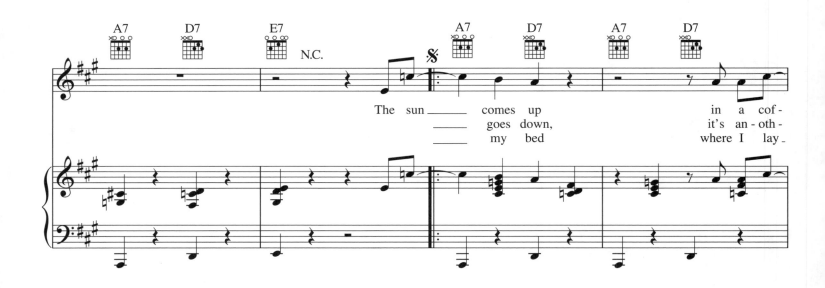

The sun _____ comes up
_____ goes down,
_____ my bed

in a cof-
it's an-oth-
where I lay _

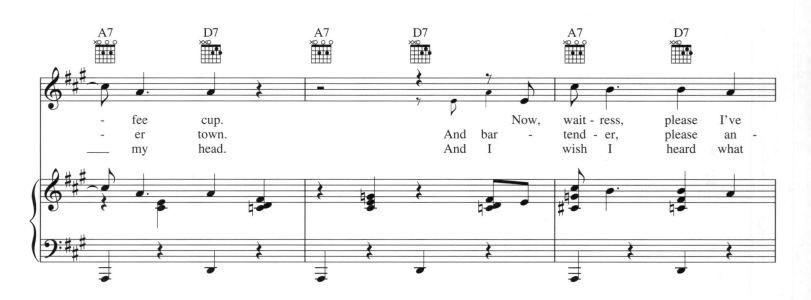

-fee   cup.
-er   town.
____ my   head.

Now,   wait-ress,   please   I've
And   bar-   tend-er,   please   an-
And   I   wish   I   heard   what

ICE CREAM

Words and Music by
SARAH McLACHLAN

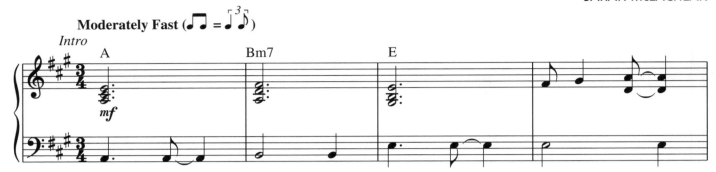

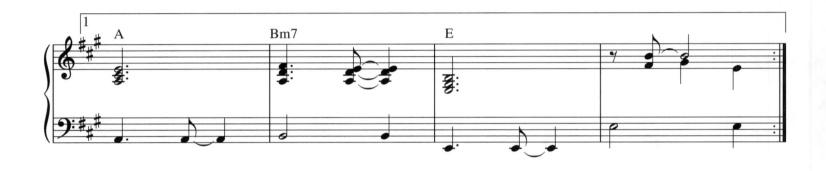

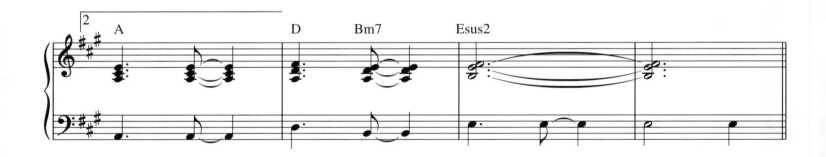

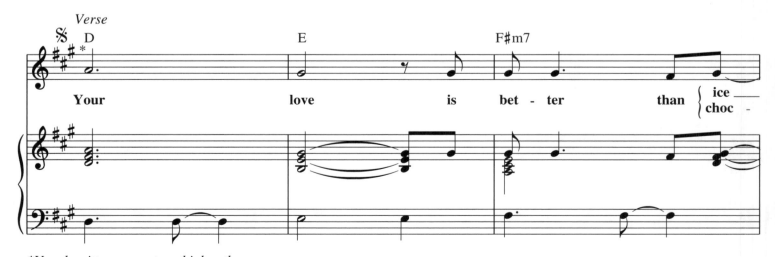

Vocal written one octave higher than sung.

IT'S A HARD LIFE WHEREVER YOU GO

Words and Music by
NANCI GRIFFITH

1. I am a back-seat driv - er from A - mer - i - ca. We
2., 3. (See additional lyrics)

drive to the left __ on Ford's road. And the man at the wheel's __ name is

Sha - mus. We pass a child on the cor - ner he knows, and

Additional Lyrics

2. Cafeteria line in Chicago;
   The fat man in front of me
   Is calling black people trash to his children,
   And he's the only trash here I see.
   And I'm thinking, this man wears a white hood
   In the night when his children should sleep;
   But they'll slip to their windows, and they'll see him,
   And they'll think that white hood's all they need.
   Chorus

3. I was a child in the Sixties,
   When dreams could be had through T.V.,
   With Disney and Cronkite and Martin Luther;
   And I believed, I believed, I believed.
   Now, I'm a back-seat driver from America,
   And I am not at the wheel of control,
   And I am guilty, and I am war, and I am the root of all evil,
   Lord, and I can't drive on the left side of the road.
   Chorus

LADY BLUE

Words and Music by
LEON RUSSELL

LAST GOODBYE

Words and Music by
JEFF BUCKLEY

gave me more ___ to live for, _____ more than you'll ev - er know. _____

Well, _____ this is ___ our last _____ em -

brace. _____ Must I dream ___ and al - ways ___ see your

face? _____   Why can't we o - ver-come this

wall? __   Ba - by, may - be it's just be - cause _ I did-n't

know you at all. _____

LET HIM FLY

Words and Music by
PATTY GRIFFIN

LONGER

Words and Music by
DAN FOGELBERG

Moderate Ballad

Long - er than ___ there've been fish - es in the o - cean,
Strong - er than ___ an - y moun - tain ca - the - dral,
Through the years ___ as the fi - re starts to mel - low,

high - er than ___ an - y bird ev - er flew, ___
tru - er than ___ an - y tree ev - er grew, ___
burn - ing lines ___ in the book of our lives, ___

Long - er than ___ there've been
Deep - er than ___ an - y
Though the bind - ing cracks ___ and the pag-

CODA

I'll be in love __ with you. __

Long-er than __ there've been

LOVE THE ONE YOU'RE WITH

Words and Music by
STEPHEN STILLS

MAKE IT WITH YOU

Words and Music by
DAVID GATES

MEMPHIS IN THE MEANTIME

Words and Music by
JOHN HIATT

Be - fore our up - per lips __ get stiff, may - be we need __

__ us a big ol' whiff.

If I could

Let's go to Mem - phis in __ the mean-

- time, ba - by.   Let's go to Mem -

- phis in ___ the mean - time, girl.   Mmm, we're talk - in' 'bout

Mem - phis.

Optional Ending

E7

Repeat and Fade

ME AND BOBBY McGEE

Words and Music by KRIS KRISTOFFERSON
and FRED FOSTER

Busted flat in Baton Rouge, waitin' for a train, when I's feelin' near as faded as my jeans. Bobby thumbed a diesel down just before it rained. It rode us all the way into New Orleans. I

* Vocal written one octave higher than sung.

Lord.

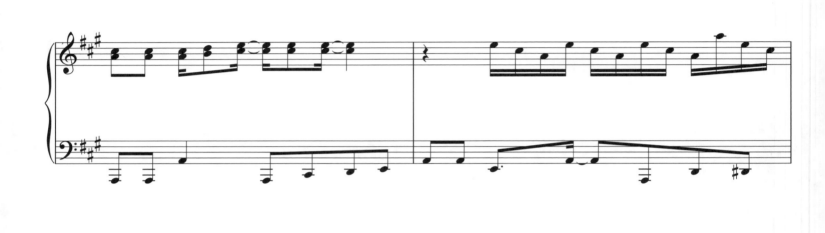

MONDAY, MONDAY

Words and Music by
JOHN PHILLIPS

be._____
way._____

Oh, Mon - day morn - in', Mon - day morn -
Oh, Mon - day, morn - in' you give me no warn -

- in' could - n't guar - an - tee_____
- in' ____ of what was to be ____

That Mon - day
Oh, Mon - day,

eve - nin' you would still be here___ with me.
Mon - day how could you still leave and not ___ take

MRS. ROBINSON

Words and Music by
PAUL SIMON

for those who pray, (Hey, hey, hey,

hey, hey, hey)

To Coda

Verse

1. We'd like to know a lit - tle bit a - bout you for our files,

We'd like to help you learn to help your - self.

254

NIGHTS IN WHITE SATIN

Words and Music by
JUSTIN HAYWARD

C
love you,
Oh, how I love you.
1 Em
D
Em
D
2 Em
love you.
D
Em
Oh, how I love
D
you.
Em
Em7
f
mp

REASON TO BELIEVE

Words and Music by
TIM HARDIN

that you ___ lied straight - faced while I cried. ___

Still I look to find a rea -

son to be - lieve. Some - one like

you makes it hard to live with - out

2. *Violin solo*

NORWEGIAN WOOD
(This Bird Has Flown)

Words and Music by JOHN LENNON
and PAUL McCARTNEY

OLIVER'S ARMY

Words and Music by
ELVIS COSTELLO

OOO BABY BABY

Words and Music by WILLIAM "SMOKEY" ROBINSON
and WARREN MOORE

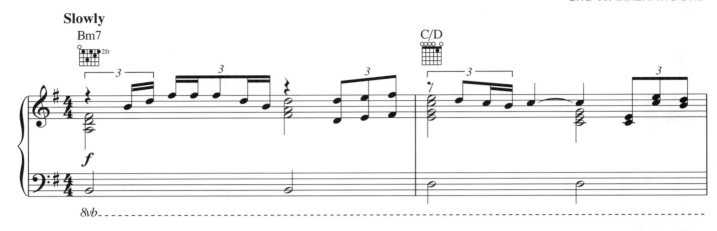

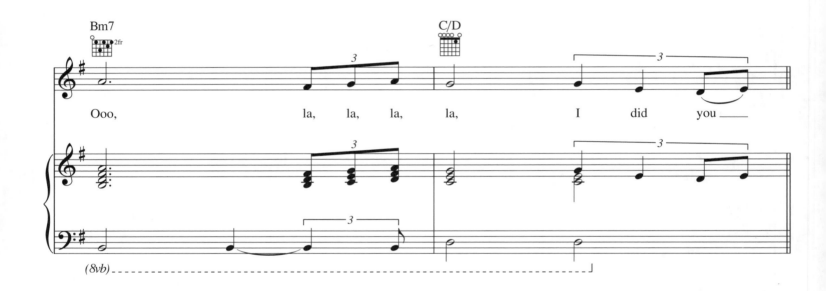

Ooo, la, la, la, la, I did you

wrong; __ my heart __ went out to play, and in the game, __ I
takes, __ I know __ I've made a few, but I'm on-ly

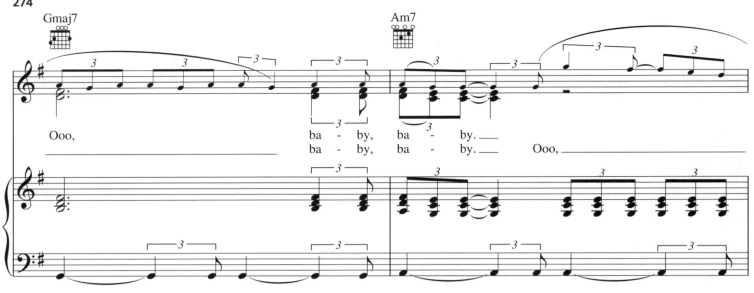

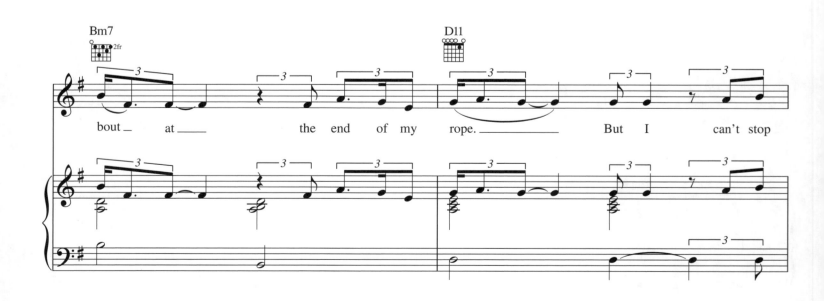

OPERATOR
(That's Not the Way It Feels)

Words and Music by
JIM CROCE

Op - er - a - tor,   could you
Op - er - a - tor,   could you
Op - er - a - tor,   let's for -

help me place __ this call? ___   You see, the num - ber on the
help me place __ this call, ___   'cause I can't read the num - ber
get a - bout __ this call; ___   there's no one there I real - ly

PERFECTLY GOOD GUITAR

Words and Music by
JOHN HIATT

Moderate Country beat

He threw one down from the top of the stairs, _
start-ed back ___ in nine-teen-six-ty-three, his
ought-a be a law with ___ no bail, _

PLEASE COME TO BOSTON

Words and Music by
DAVE LOGGINS

He said please come to Bos - ton for _ the spring -
please come to Den - ver with _ the snow -
please come to L. A. _ to live _ for - ev -

- time.   I'm stay - ing here _ with some friends _
- fall.   We'll move up in - to the moun -
- er.   A Cal - i - for - nia life _

Repeat and Fade

THE ROAD GOES ON FOREVER

Words and Music by
ROBERT EARL KEEN

Moderately fast

1. Sher-ry was _ a wait-ress at the on-ly joint _ in town. She
2. Son-ny was _ a lon-er, old-er than _ the rest. He was
3. Son-ny's play-in' eight-ball at the joint _ where Sher-ry works, when some
4.-7. *(See additional lyrics)*

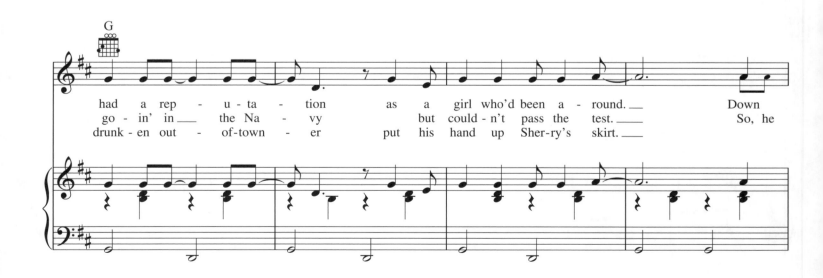

had a rep-u-ta-tion as a girl who'd been a-round. _ Down
go-in' in _ the Na-vy but could-n't pass the test. _ So, he
drunk-en out-of-town-er put his hand up Sher-ry's skirt. _

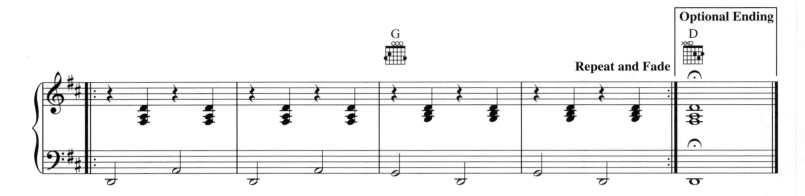

Additional Lyrics

4. They jumped into his pickup, Sonny jammed her down in gear.
Sonny looked at Sherry, said, "Let's get on out of here."
The stars were high above them, the moon was in the east.
The sun was setting on them when they reached Miami Beach.
They got a motel by the water and a quart of Bombay Gin.
The road goes on forever and the party never ends.

5. They soon ran out of money, but Sonny knew a man
Who knew some Cuban refugees that dealt in contraband.
Sonny met the Cubans in a house just off the route,
With a briefcase full of money and a pistol in his boot.
The cards were on the table when the law came busting in.
The road goes on forever and the party never ends.

6. The Cubans grabbed the goodies, Sonny grabbed the jack.
He broke the bathroom window and climbed on out the back.
Sherry drove the pickup through the alley on the side
Where a lawman tackled Sonny and was reading him his rights.
She stepped out in the alley with a single-shot four-ten.
The road goes on forever and the party never ends.

7. They left the lawman lying, they made their getaway,
Got back to the motel just before the break of day.
Sonny gave her all the money and he blew a little kiss.
"If they ask you how this happened, say I forced you into this."
She watched him as the taillights disappeared around the bend.
The road goes on forever and the party never ends.

SARA SMILE

Words and Music by DARYL HALL
and JOHN OATES

SAME OLD LANG SYNE

Words and Music by
DAN FOGELBERG

1. Met my old lov-er in the groc-'ry store. _____
2. She did-n't rec-og-nize the face at first, _____
3. *Instrumental*----------
4. We took her groc-'ries to the check-out stand; _____
5. We went to have our-selves a drink or two, _____
6. She said she's mar-ried her an arch-i-tect, _____
7. I said the years had been a friend to her _____
8. She said she saw me in the rec-ord stores, _____

*Play F♯ on verses 1, 2 and 3; play D on verses 4 - 8 (the chord on 4 - 8 is D9)

SCOTCH AND SODA

Words and Music by
DAVE GUARD

SOMEBODY TO LOVE

Words and Music by
DARBY SLICK

With a steady beat

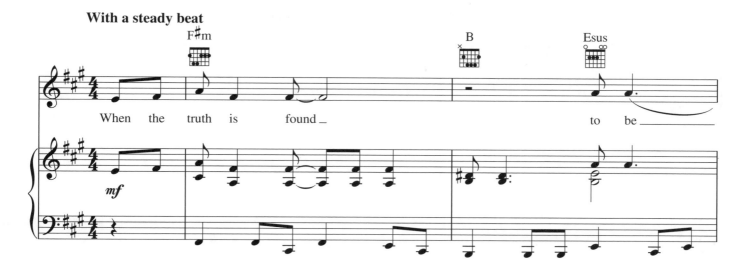

When the truth is found _ to be _

_ lies, and all _ the joy _

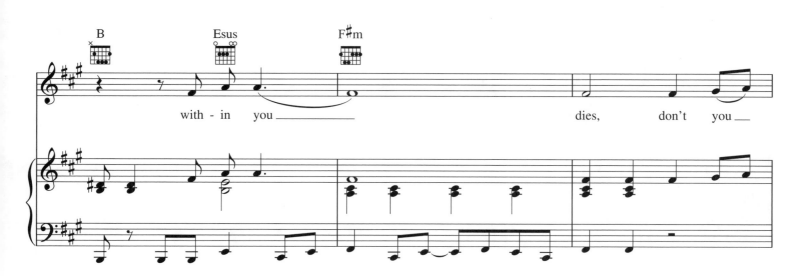

with - in you _ dies, don't you _

SENTIMENTAL LADY

Words and Music by
ROBERT WELCH

SILVER THREADS AND GOLDEN NEEDLES

Words and Music by DICK REYNOLDS
and JACK RHODES

I don't want your lone- ly man- sion with a tear ___ in ev- 'ry room. ___ All I want's the love ___ you prom- ised ___ be- neath the ha- lo'd

SUNSHINE
(GO AWAY TODAY)

Written by
JONATHAN EDWARDS

Moderately

Sun-shine go ___ a - way to-day, ___ I don't feel much ___ like ___
Sun-shine go ___ a - way to-day, ___ I don't feel much ___ like ___

danc - in'. ___ Some man's gone ___ and tried to run my ___ life. ___ He
danc - in'. ___ Some man's gone ___ and tried to run my ___ life. ___ He

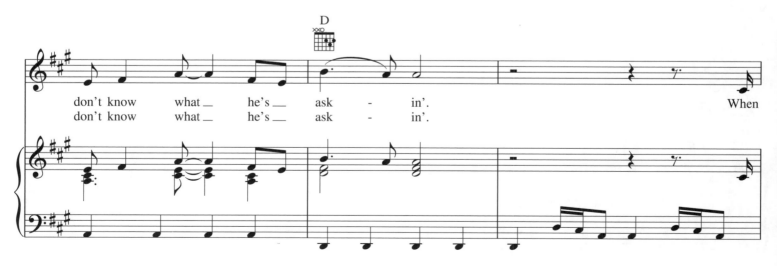

don't know what ___ he's ___ ask - in'.
don't know what ___ he's ___ ask - in'. When

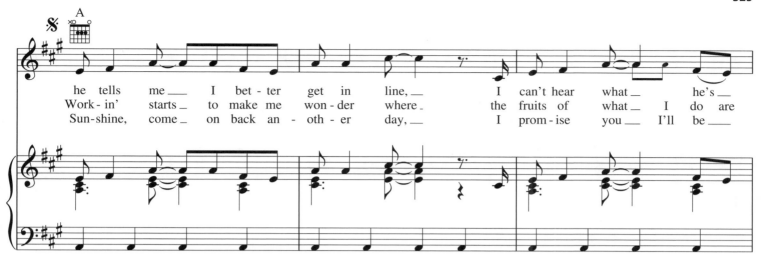

he tells me ___ I bet-ter get in line, ___ I can't hear what __ he's __
Work-in' starts __ to make me won-der where __ the fruits of what __ I do are
Sun-shine, come __ on back an - oth - er day, __ I prom-ise you __ I'll be __

say - in'. When I grow up, ___ I'm gon-na make it mine, ___ or
go - in'. He says in love __ and war __ all is fair, ___ but
sing - in'. This old world, __ she's gon-na turn a - round; __

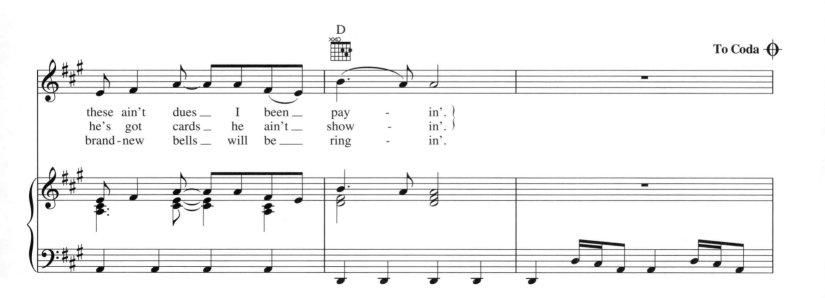

these ain't dues __ I been __ pay - in'.
he's got cards __ he ain't __ show - in'.
brand-new bells __ will be ___ ring - in'.

To Coda ⊕

SUNSHINE SUPERMAN

Words and Music by
DONOVAN LEITCH

Moderately, with a beat

Sun - shine___ came soft - ly through my (a)-win-dow to - day,___
Ev - 'ry-bod-y's hust - lin' just to have a lit - tle___ scene___

Su - per - man or Green Lan - tern ain't ___ got

(a)-noth -in' on me, ___ I can make like a tur -

- tle and dive for pearls in the sea; ___

I'll pick up your hand___ and slow - ly

blow your lit - tle mind,___ When you've made your

mind up for - ev - er to be mine.___

Repeat and fade

SUZANNE

Words and Music by
LEONARD COHEN

think   you may - be   trust her,___ 'Cause she's touched your per-fect bod-y,_____ with her
think   you may - be   trust Him,___ For   he's touched your per-fect bod-y,_____ with His
think   may-be you'll trust her,___ For you've touched her per-fect bod-y,_____ with your

1.2.

mind._____   2. And
mind._____   3. Suz -

3.

mind._____

ritard

TANGLED UP IN BLUE

Words and Music by
BOB DYLAN

1. Ear-ly one morn-in' the sun __ was shin-in', I was lay-in' in bed, __
2. She __ was mar-ried when we __ first met, soon to be __ di-vorced. __
3. I had a job in the great __ North woods, work-in' as a cook for a spell. __ But I

4.-7. *(See additional lyrics)*
8. *Instrumental*

won-d'rin' if __ she's changed at all, __ if her hair was __ still red. __
I helped her out of a jam, I guess, __ but I used a lit-tle too much force. We
nev-er did like __ it all that much __ and one day the axe just fell. __ So I

Tan - gled up in blue.___
tan - gled up in blue.___

Additional Lyrics

4. She was working in topless place
   And I stopped in for a beer.
   I just kept looking at the side of her face
   In the spotlight so clear.
   And later on when the crowd thinned out
   I was just about to do the same.
   She was standing there in back of my chair,
   Said to me, "Don't I know your name?"
   I muttered something underneath my breath.
   She studied the lines on my face.
   I must admit I felt a little uneasy
   When she bent down to tie the laces of my shoe,
   Tangled up in blue.

5. She lit a burner on the stove
   And offered me a pipe.
   "I thought you'd never say hello," she said.
   "You look like the silent type."
   Then she opened up a book of poems
   And handed it to me,
   Written by an Italian poet
   From the thirteenth century.
   And every one of them words rang true
   And glowed like burning coal,
   Pourin' off of every page
   Like it was written in my soul,
   From me to you,
   Tangled up in blue.

6. I lived with them on Montague Street
   In a basement down the stairs.
   There was music in the cafes at night
   And revolution in the air.
   Then he started in the dealing in slaves
   And something inside of him died.
   She had to sell everything she owned
   And froze up inside.
   And when finally the bottom finally fell out
   I became withdrawn.
   The only thing I knew how to do
   Was to keep on keeping on,
   Like a bird that flew
   Tangled up in blue.

7. So now I'm going back again.
   I got to get to her somehow.
   All the people we used to know,
   They're an illusion to me now.
   Some are mathematicians,
   Some are carpenter's wives.
   Don't know how it all got started,
   I don't know what they do with their lives.
   But me, I'm still on the road
   Headin' for another joint.
   We always did feel the same,
   We just saw it from a different point of view,
   Tangled up in blue.

THERE'S A LIGHT BEYOND THESE WOODS

Words and Music by
NANCI GRIFFITH

Moderately slow, in 2

2. Have you met my ___ new

3., 4. *(See additional lyrics)*

boy - friend, Mar - garet?

His name ___ is John, ___ and he rides ___ my bus to school, ___

___ and he holds _____ my hand. _____

There'll ___ nev - er be ___ two friends _____ like you and me, ___ Mar - y Mar - garet. _____

There's a light be - yond ___ your woods, _____ Mar - y

Mar - garet...

rit. e dim.

Additional Lyrics

3. Let's go to New York City, Margaret.
   We'll hide out in the subways and drink the poet's wine.
   Oh, but I had John;
   So you went and I stayed behind.
   But you were home in time for the Senior Prom,
   When we lost John.
   (To bridge 1:)

4. It's nice to see your family growing, Margaret;
   Your daughter and your husband here, they really treat you right,
   But we've talked all night;
   What about those lights
   That glowed beyond our woods when we were ten?
   You were the rambler then.
   (To bridge 2:)

Bridge 2. The fantasies we planned, oh Maggie I'm livin' 'em now.
   All the dreams we sang, well, we damn sure knew how.
   But I'll never change,
   And there'll never be two friends just like you and me,
   Maggie, can't you see?
   There's a light beyond your woods, Mary Margaret...

THIS SHIRT

Words and Music by
MARY CHAPIN CARPENTER

*Vocal is written 8va higher than sung.

TIME IN A BOTTLE

Words and Music by
JIM CROCE

THE TRACKS OF MY TEARS

Words and Music by WILLIAM "SMOKEY" ROBINSON,
WARREN MOORE and MARVIN TARPLIN

THE UNIVERSAL SOLDIER

Words and Music by
BUFFY SAINT-MARIE

VINCENT
(Starry Starry Night)

Words and Music by
DON McLEAN

372

YOU WERE MEANT FOR ME

Words and Music by JEWEL KILCHER
and STEVE POLTZ

WE JUST DISAGREE

Words and Music by
JIM KRUEGER

YOU'VE GOT A FRIEND

Words and Music by
CAROLE KING

*Vocal harmony sung 2nd time only.

YOU'VE GOT TO HIDE YOUR LOVE AWAY

Words and Music by JOHN LENNON
and PAUL McCARTNEY

Moderately, (in 2)

YOU'RE ONLY LONELY

Words and Music by
JOHN DAVID SOUTHER